THE
PRINCE OF PEACE

By

WILLIAM JENNINGS BRYAN

FUNK & WAGNALLS COMPANY

NEW YORK AND LONDON

1914

PUBLISHERS' NOTE

"The Prince of Peace" is a lecture delivered by Mr. Bryan at many Chautauquas and religious gatherings in America, beginning in 1904; also in Canada, Mexico, Tokyo, Manila, Bombay, Cairo and Jerusalem.

Published, September, 1914

THE PRINCE OF PEACE

I OFFER no apology for speaking upon a religious theme, for it is the most universal of all themes. The science of government is interesting, but I am more interested in religion than in government. Making a political speech is enjoyable—I have made a good many and shall make more—but I would rather speak on religion than on politics. I commenced speaking on the stump when only twenty, but commenced speaking in the church six weeks earlier—and shall be in the church even after I am out of politics. I feel sure of my ground when making a political speech, but am more certain of my ground when making a religious speech. If this address were upon the subject of law, the lawyers might be interested; if upon the science of medicine, it might interest the physicians; in like manner merchants might be interested in comments on commerce, and farmers in matters pertaining to agriculture; but no one of these subjects appeals to all. Even the science of government, tho broader than any profession or occupation, does not embrace the whole sum of life, and those who think upon it differ so among themselves that one could not speak upon the subject so as to please a part of the audience without displeasing others. While to me the science of government is intensely absorbing, I recognize that the most important things in life lie outside of the realm of government and that more de-

[4]

pends upon what the individual does for himself than upon what the government does or can do for him. Men can be miserable under the best government and they can be happy under the worst government.

Government affects but a part of the life which we live here and does not deal at all with the life beyond, while religion touches the infinite circle of existence as well as the small arc of that circle which we spend on earth. No greater theme, therefore, can engage our attention. When discussing questions of government I must secure the cooperation of a majority before my ideas can be put into practise, but if, in speaking on religion, I can touch one human heart for good, I have not spoken in vain no matter how large the majority may be against me.

[5]

THE PRINCE OF PEACE

Man is a religious being; the heart instinctively seeks for a God. Whether he worships on the banks of the Ganges, prays with his face upturned to the sun, kneels toward Mecca or, regarding all space as a temple, communes with the Heavenly Father according to the Christian creed, man is essentially devout.

There are honest doubters whose sincerity we recognize and respect, but occasionally I find young men who think it smart to be skeptical; they talk as if it were an evidence of larger intelligence to scoff at creeds and to refuse to connect themselves with churches. They call themselves "liberal," as if a Christian were narrow minded. Some go so far as to assert that the "advanced thought of the world" has discarded the idea that there is a God. To these young men I desire to address myself.

Even some older people profess to regard religion as a superstition, pardonable in the ignorant but unworthy of the educated. Those who hold this view look down with mild contempt upon such as give to religion a definite place in their thoughts and lives. They assume an intellectual superiority and often take little pains to conceal the assumption. Tolstoy administers to the "cultured crowd" (the words quoted are his) a severe rebuke when he declares that the religious sentiment rests not upon a superstitious fear of the invisible forces of nature, but upon man's consciousness of his finiteness amid an infinite universe and of his sinfulness; and this consciousness, the great philosopher adds, man can

never outgrow. Tolstoy is right;
man recognizes how limited are his
own powers and how vast is the universe, and he leans upon the Arm that
is stronger than his. Man feels the
weight of his sins and looks for One
who is sinless.

Religion has been defined by Tolstoy as the relation which man fixes
between himself and his God, and
morality as the outward manifesta-
tion of this inward relation. Every
one, by the time he reaches maturity,
has fixt some relation between himself and God and no material change
in this relation can take place without
a revolution in the man, for this relation is the most potent influence that
acts upon a human life.

Religion is the foundation of morality in the individual and in the
group of individuals. Materialists

have attempted to build up a system
of morality upon the basis of enlight-
ened self-interest. They would have
man figure out by mathematics that
it pays him to abstain from wrong-
doing; they would even inject an element of selfishness into altruism, but
the moral system elaborated by the
materialists has several defects.
First, its virtues are borrowed from
moral systems based upon religion.
All those who are intelligent enough
to discuss a system of morality are
so saturated with the morals derived
from systems resting upon religion
that they can not frame a system resting upon reason alone. Second, as
it rests upon argument rather than
upon authority, the young are not in
a position to accept or reject. Our
laws do not permit a young man to
dispose of real estate until he is twen-

ty-one. Why this restraint? Because his reason is not mature; and yet a man's life is largely molded by the environment of his youth. Third, one never knows just how much of his decision is due to reason and how much is due to passion or to selfish interest. Passion can dethrone the reason—we recognize this in our criminal laws. We also recognize the bias of self-interest when we exclude from the jury every man, no matter how reasonable or upright he may be, who has a pecuniary interest in the result of the trial. And, fourth, one whose morality rests upon a nice calculation of benefits to be secured spends time in figuring that he should spend in action. Those who keep a book account of their good deeds seldom do enough good to justify keeping books. A noble life can not be built upon an arithmetic; it must be rather like the spring that pours forth constantly that which refreshes and invigorates.

Morality is the power of endurance in man; and a religion which teaches personal responsibility to God gives strength to morality. There is a powerful restraining influence in the belief that an all-seeing eye scrutinizes every thought and word and act of the individual.

There is wide difference between the man who is trying to conform his life to a standard of morality about him and the man who seeks to make his life approximate to a divine standard. The former attempts to live up to the standard, if it is above him, and down to it, if it is below him—and if he is doing right only when others are looking he is sure to find a time when he thinks he is unobserved, and then he takes a vacation and falls. One needs the inner strength which comes with the conscious presence of a personal God. If those who are thus fortified sometimes yield to temptation, how helpless and hopeless must those be who rely upon their own strength alone!

There are difficulties to be encountered in religion, but there are difficulties to be encountered everywhere. If Christians sometimes have doubts and fears, unbelievers have more doubts and greater fears. I passed through a period of skepticism when I was in college and I have been glad ever since that I became a member of the church before I left home for college, for it helped me during those trying days. And the college days cover the dangerous period in the young man's life; he is just coming into possession of his powers, and feels stronger than he ever feels afterward—and he thinks he knows more than he ever does know.

It was at this period that I became confused by the different theories of creation. But I examined these theories and found that they all assumed something to begin with. You can test this for yourselves. The nebular hypothesis, for instance, assumes that matter and force existed—matter in particles infinitely fine and each particle separated from every other particle by space infinitely great. Beginning with this assumption, force working on matter—according to this hypothesis—created a universe. I have as much right to assume as they, and I prefer to assume, a Designer back of the design—a Creator back of the creation; and no matter how long you draw out the process of creation, so long as God stands back of it you cannot shake my faith in Jehovah. In Genesis it is written that, in the beginning, God created the heavens and the earth, and I can stand on that proposition until I find some theory of creation that goes farther back than "the beginning." We must begin with something—we must start somewhere—and the Christian begins with God.

I do not carry the doctrine of evolution as far as some do; I am not yet convinced that man is a lineal descendant of the lower animals. I do not mean to find fault with you if you want to accept the theory; all I mean to say is that while you may trace your ancestry back to the monkey if you find pleasure or pride in doing so, you shall not connect me with your family tree without more evidence than has yet been produced. I object to the theory for several reasons. First, it is a dangerous theory. If a man links himself in generations with the monkey, it then becomes an important question whether he is going toward him or coming from him —and I have seen them going in both directions. I do not know of any argument that can be used to prove that man is an improved monkey that may not be used just as well to prove that the monkey is a degenerate man, and the latter theory is more plausible than the former.

It is true that man, in some physical characteristics resembles the beast, but man has a mind as well as a body, and a soul as well as a mind. The mind is greater than the body

[15]

and the soul is greater than the mind, and I object to having man's pedigree traced on one-third of him only— and that the lowest third. Fairbairn, in his "Philosophy of Christianity," lays down a sound proposition when he says that it is not sufficient to explain man as an animal; that it is necessary to explain man in history —and the Darwinian theory does not do this. The ape, according to this theory, is older than man and yet the ape is still an ape while man is the author of the marvelous civilization which we see about us.

One does not escape from mystery, however, by accepting this theory, for it does not explain the origin of life. When the follower of Darwin has traced the germ of life back to the lowest form in which it appears—and to follow him one must exercise more

faith than religion calls for—he finds
that scientists differ. Those who reject the idea of creation are divided
into two schools, some believing that
the first germ of life came from another planet and others holding that
it was the result of spontaneous generation. Each school answers the
arguments advanced by the other,
and as they can not agree with each
other, I am not compelled to agree
with either.

If I were compelled to accept one
of these theories I would prefer the
first, for if we can chase the germ of
life off this planet and get it out into
space we can guess the rest of the
way and no one can contradict us, but
if we accept the doctrine of spontaneous generation we can not explain
why spontaneous generation ceased

to act after the first germ was
created.

Go back as far as we may, we can
not escape from the creative act, and
it is just as easy for me to believe
that God created man *as he is* as to
believe that, millions of years ago, He
created a germ of life and endowed
it with power to develop into all that
we see to-day. I object to the Darwinian theory, until more conclusive
proof is produced, because I fear we
shall lose the consciousness of God's
presence in our daily life, if we must
accept the theory that through all the
ages no spiritual force has touched
the life of man or shaped the destiny
of nations.

But there is another objection.
The Darwinian theory represents
man as reaching his present perfec-
tion by the operation of the law of

hate—the merciless law by which the strong crowd out and kill off the weak. If this is the law of our development then, if there is any logic that can bind the human mind, we shall turn backward toward the beast in proportion as we substitute the law of love. I prefer to believe that love rather than hatred is the law of development. How can hatred be the law of development when nations have advanced in proportion as they have departed from that law and adopted the law of love?

But, I repeat, while I do not accept the Darwinian theory I shall not quarrel with you about it; I only refer to it to remind you that it does not solve the mystery of life or explain human progress. I fear that some have accepted it in the hope of escaping from the miracle, but why should the miracle frighten us? And yet I am inclined to think that it is one of the test questions with the Christian.

Christ can not be separated from the miraculous; His birth, His ministrations, and His resurrection, all involve the miraculous, and the change which His religion works in the human heart is a continuing miracle. Eliminate the miracles and Christ becomes merely a human being and His gospel is stript of divine authority.

The miracle raises two questions: "Can God perform a miracle?" and, "Would He want to?" The first is easy to answer. A God who can make a world can do anything He wants to do with it. The power to perform miracles is necessarily implied in the power to create. But

[20]

would God *want* to perform a miracle?—this is the question which has given most of the trouble. The more I have considered it the less inclined I am to answer in the negative. To say that God *would not* perform a miracle is to assume a more intimate knowledge of God's plans and purposes than I can claim to have. I will not deny that God does perform a miracle or may perform one merely because I do not know how or why He does it. I find it so difficult to decide each day what God wants done now that I am not presumptuous enough to attempt to declare what God might have wanted to do thousands of years ago. The fact that we are constantly learning of the existence of new forces suggests the possibility that God may operate through forces yet unknown to us,

[21]

and the mysteries with which we deal every-day warn me that faith is as necessary as sight. Who would have credited a century ago the stories that are now told of the wonder-working electricity? For ages man had known the lightning, but only to fear it; now, this invisible current is generated by a man-made machine, imprisoned in a man-made wire and made to do the bidding of man. We are even able to dispense with the wire and hurl words through space, and the X-ray has enabled us to look through substances which were supposed, until recently, to exclude all light. The miracle is not more mysterious than many of the things with which man now deals—it is simply different. The miraculous birth of Christ is not more mysterious than any other conception—it is simply unlike it; nor is the resurrection of Christ more mysterious than the myriad resurrections which mark each annual seed-time.

It is sometimes said that God could not suspend one of His laws without stopping the universe, but do we not suspend or overcome the law of gravitation every-day? Every time we move a foot or lift a weight we temporarily overcome one of the most universal of natural laws and yet the world is not disturbed.

Science has taught us so many things that we are tempted to conclude that we know everything, but there is really a great unknown which is still unexplored and that which we have learned ought to increase our reverence rather than our egotism. Science has disclosed some of the machinery of the universe, but science has not yet revealed to us the great secret—the secret of life. It is to be found in every blade of grass, in every insect, in every bird and in every animal, as well as in man. Six thousand years of recorded history and yet we know no more about the secret of life than they knew in the beginning. We live, we plan; we have our hopes, our fears; and yet in a moment a change may come over anyone of us and this body will become a mass of lifeless clay. What is it that, having, we live, and having not, we are as the clod? The progress of the race and the civilization which we now behold are the work of men and women who have not yet solved the mystery of their own lives.

And our food, must we understand it before we eat it? If we refused to eat anything until we could understand the mystery of its growth, we would die of starvation. But mystery does not bother us in the dining-room; it is only in the church that it is a stumbling block.

I was eating a piece of watermelon some months ago and was struck with its beauty. I took some of the seeds and dried them and weighed them, and found that it would require some five thousand seeds to weigh a pound; and then I applied mathematics to that forty-pound melon. One of these seeds, put into the ground, when warmed by the sun and moistened by the rain, takes off its coat and goes to work; it gathers from somewhere two hundred thousand times its own weight, and forcing this raw material through a tiny stem, constructs a watermelon. It ornaments the outside with a covering of green; inside the green it puts a layer of white, and within the white a core of red, and all through the red it scatters seeds, each one capable of continuing the work of reproduction. Who drew the plan by which that little seed works? Where does it get its tremendous strength? Where does it find its coloring matter? How does it collect its flavoring extract? How does it develop a watermelon? Until you can explain a watermelon, do not be too sure that you can set limits to the power of the Almighty and say just what He would do or how He would do it.

The egg is the most universal of foods and its use dates from the beginning, but what is more mysterious than an egg? When an egg is fresh it is an important article of merchandise; a hen can destroy its market value in a week's time, but in two weeks more she can bring forth from it what man could not find in it. We eat eggs, but we can not explain an egg.

Water has been used from the birth of man; we learned after it had been used for ages that it is merely a mixture of gases, but it is far more important that we have water to drink than that we know that it is not water.

Everything that grows tells a like story of infinite power. Why should I deny that a divine hand fed a multitude with a few loaves and fishes when I see hundreds of millions fed every year by a hand which converts the seeds scattered over the field into an abundant harvest? We know that food can be multiplied in a few

[27]

months' time; shall we deny the power of the Creator to eliminate the element of time, when we have gone so far in eliminating the element of space? Who am I that I should attempt to measure the arm of the Almighty with my puny arm, or to measure the brain of the Infinite with my finite mind? Who am I that I should attempt to put metes and bounds to the power of the Creator?

But there is something even more wonderful still — the mysterious change that takes place in the human heart when the man begins to hate the things he loved and to love the things he hated — the marvelous transformation that takes place in the man who, before the change, would have sacrificed a world for his own advancement but who, after the change, would give his

life for a principle and esteem
it a privilege to make sacrifice for his convictions! What
greater miracle than this, that converts a selfish, self-centered, human
being into a center from which good
influences flow out in every direction!
And yet this miracle has been
wrought in the heart of each one of
us—or may be wrought — and we
have seen it wrought in the hearts
and lives of those about us. No, living a life that is a mystery, and living in the midst of mystery and miracles, I shall not allow either to de-
prive me of the benefits of the
Christian religion. If you ask me if
I understand everything in the Bible,
I answer, no, but if we will try to
live up to what we do understand, we
will be kept so busy doing good that
we will not have time to worry about

the passages which we do not understand.

Some of those who question the miracle also question the theory of atonement; they assert that it does not accord with their idea of justice for one to die for all. Let each one bear his own sins and the punishments due for them, they say. The doctrine of vicarious suffering is not a new one; it is as old as the race. That one should suffer for others is one of the most familiar of principles and we see the principle illustrated every-day of our lives. Take the family, for instance; from the day the mother's first child is born, for twenty or thirty years her children are scarcely out of her waking thoughts. Her life trembles in the balance at each child's birth; she sacrifices for them, she surrenders herself to them. Is it because she expects them to pay her back? Fortunate for the parent and fortunate for the child if the latter has an opportunity to repay in part the debt it owes. But no child can compensate a parent for a parent's care. In the course of nature the debt is paid, not to the parent, but to the next generation, and the next—each generation suffering, sacrificing for and surrendering itself to the generation that follows. This is the law of our lives.

Nor is this confined to the family. Every step in civilization has been made possible by those who have been willing to sacrifice for posterity. Freedom of speech, freedom of the press, freedom of conscience and free government have all been won for the world by those who were willing to labor unselfishly for their fellows.

[31]

So well established is this doctrine
that we do not regard anyone as
great unless he recognizes how unim-
portant his life is in comparison with
the problems with which he deals.

I find proof that man was made in
the image of his Creator in the fact
that, throughout the centuries, man
has been willing to die, if necessary,
that blessings denied to him might be
enjoyed by his children, his children's
children and the world.

The seeming paradox: "He that
saveth his life shall lose it and he that
loseth his life for my sake shall find
it," has an application wider than
that usually given to it; it is an epit-
ome of history. Those who live only
for themselves live little lives, but
those who stand ready to give themselves for the advancement of things
greater than themselves find a larger

life than the one they would have surrendered. Wendell Phillips gave expression to the same idea when he said, "What imprudent men the benefactors of the race have been. How prudently most men sink into nameless graves, while now and then a few *forget* themselves into immortality." We win immortality, not by remembering ourselves, but by forgetting ourselves in devotion to things larger than ourselves.

Instead of being an unnatural plan, the plan of salvation is in perfect harmony with human nature as we understand it. Sacrifice is the language of love, and Christ, in suffering for the world, adopted the only means of reaching the heart. This can be demonstrated not only by theory but by experience, for the story of His life, His teachings, His sufferings and His death has been translated into every language and everywhere it has touched the heart.

But if I were going to present an argument in favor of the divinity of Christ, I would not begin with miracles or mystery or with the theory of atonement. I would begin as Carnegie Simpson does in his book entitled, "The Fact of Christ." Commencing with the undisputed fact that Christ lived, he points out that one can not contemplate this fact without feeling that in some way it is related to those now living. He says that one can read of Alexander, of Cæsar or of Napoleon, and not feel that it is a matter of personal concern; but that when one reads that Christ lived, and how He lived and how He died, he feels that somehow there is a cord that stretches from that life to his. As he studies the character of Christ he becomes conscious of certain virtues which stand out in bold relief—His purity, His forgiving spirit, and His unfathomable love. The author is correct. Christ presents an example of purity in thought and life, and man, conscious of his own imperfections and grieved over his shortcomings, finds inspiration in the fact that He was tempted in all points like as we are, and yet without sin. I am not sure but that each can find just here a way of determining for himself whether he possesses the true spirit of a Christian. If the sinlessness of Christ inspires within him an earnest desire to conform his life more nearly to the perfect example, he is indeed a follower; if, on the other hand, he resents the reproof which the purity of Christ offers, and refuses to mend his ways, he has yet to be born again.

The most difficult of all the virtues to cultivate is the forgiving spirit. Revenge seems to be natural with man; it is human to want to get even with an enemy. It has even been popular to boast of vindictiveness; it was once inscribed on a man's monument that he had repaid both friends and enemies more than he had received. This was not the spirit of Christ. He taught forgiveness and in that incomparable prayer which He left as a model for our petitions, He made our willingness to forgive the measure by which we may claim forgiveness. He not only taught forgiveness but He exemplified His teachings in His life. When those who persecuted Him brought Him to the most disgraceful of all deaths,

His spirit of forgiveness rose above His sufferings and He prayed, "Father, forgive them, for they know not what they do!"

But love is the foundation of Christ's creed. The world had known love before; parents had loved their children, and children their parents; husbands had loved their wives, and wives their husbands; and friend had loved friend; but Jesus gave a new definition of love. His love was as wide as the sea; its limits were so far-flung that even an enemy could not travel beyond its bounds. Other teachers sought to regulate the lives of their followers by rule and formula, but Christ's plan was to purify the heart and then to leave love to direct the footsteps.

What conclusion is to be drawn from the life, the teachings and the death of this historic figure? Reared in a carpenter shop; with no knowledge of literature, save Bible literature; with no acquaintance with philosophers living or with the writings of sages dead, when only about thirty years old He gathered disciples about Him, promulgated a higher code of morals than the world had ever known before, and proclaimed Himself the Messiah. He taught and performed miracles for a few brief months and then was crucified; His disciples were scattered and many of them put to death; His claims were disputed, His resurrection denied and His followers persecuted; and yet from this beginning His religion spread until hundreds of millions have taken His name with reverence upon their lips and millions have been willing to die rather than surrender the faith which He put into their hearts. How shall we account for Him? Here is the greatest fact of history; here is One who has with increasing power, for nineteen hundred years, molded the hearts, the thoughts and the lives of men, and He exerts more influence to-day than ever before. "What think ye of Christ?" It is easier to believe Him divine than to explain in any other way what he said and did and was. And I have greater faith, even than before, since I have visited the Orient and witnessed the successful contest which Christianity is waging against the religions and philosophies of the East.

I was thinking a few years ago of the Christmas which was then approaching and of Him in whose honor the day is celebrated. I re-

called the message, "Peace on earth,
good will to men," and then my
thoughts ran back to the prophecy
uttered centuries before His birth, in
which He was described as the Prince
of Peace. To reinforce my memory
I re-read the prophecy and I found
immediately following a verse which
I had forgotten—a verse which declares that of the increase of His
peace and government there shall be
no end. And, Isaiah adds, that He
shall judge His people with justice
and with judgment. I had been read-
ing of the rise and fall of nations,
and occasionally I had met a gloomy
philosopher who preached the doctrine that nations, like individuals,
must of necessity have their birth,
their infancy, their maturity and
finally their decay and death. But
here I read of a government that is

[40]

to be perpetual—a government of increasing peace and blessedness—the government of the Prince of Peace—and it is to rest on justice. I have thought of this prophecy many times during the last few years, and I have selected this theme that I might present some of the reasons which lead me to believe that Christ has fully earned the right to be called the Prince of Peace—a title that will in the years to come be more and more applied to Him. If he can bring peace to each individual heart, and if His creed when applied will bring peace throughout the earth, who will deny His right to be called the Prince of Peace?

All the world is in search of peace; every heart that ever beat has sought for peace, and many have been the methods employed to secure it. Some

[41]

have thought to purchase it with riches and have labored to secure wealth, hoping to find peace when they were able to go where they pleased and buy what they liked. Of those who have endeavored to purchase peace with money, the large majority have failed to secure the money. But what has been the experience of those who have been eminently successful in finance? They all tell the same story, viz., that they spent the first half of their lives trying to get money from others and the last half trying to keep others from getting their money, and that they found peace in neither half. Some have even reached the point where they find difficulty in getting people to accept their money; and I know of no better indication of the ethical

[42]

awakening in this country than the increasing tendency to scrutinize the methods of money-making. I am sanguine enough to believe that the time will yet come when respectability will no longer be sold to great criminals by helping them to spend their ill-gotten gains. A long step in advance will have been taken when religious, educational and charitable institutions refuse to condone conscienceless methods in business and leave the possessor of illegitimate accumulations to learn how lonely life is when one prefers money to morals.

Some have sought peace in social distinction, but whether they have been within the charmed circle and fearful lest they might fall out, or outside, and hopeful that they might get in, they have not found peace.

Some have thought, vain thought, to find peace in political prominence; but whether office comes by birth, as in monarchies, or by election, as in republics, it does not bring peace. An office is not considered a high one if all can occupy it. Only when few in a generation can hope to enjoy an honor do we call it a great honor. I am glad that our Heavenly Father did not make the peace of the human heart to depend upon our ability to buy it with money, secure it in society, or win it at the polls, for in either case but few could have obtained it, but when He made peace the reward of a conscience void of offense toward God and man, He put it within the reach of all. The poor can secure it as easily as the rich, the social outcasts as freely as the leader of society,

[44]

and the humblest citizen equally with those who wield political power.

To those who have grown gray in the church, I need not speak of the peace to be found in faith in God and trust in an overruling Providence. Christ taught that our lives are precious in the sight of God, and poets have taken up the thought and woven it into immortal verse. No uninspired writer has exprest it more beautifully than William Cullen Bryant in his Ode to a Waterfowl. After following the wanderings of the bird of passage as it seeks first its southern and then its northern home, he concludes:

Thou art gone; the abyss of heaven
  Hath swallowed up thy form, but on my
    heart
Deeply hath sunk the lesson thou hast
    given,
  And shall not soon depart.

[45]

THE PRINCE OF PEACE

He who, from zone to zone,
  Guides through the boundless sky thy
    certain flight,
In the long way that I must tread alone,
  Will lead my steps aright.

Christ promoted peace by giving us
assurance that a line of communica-
tion can be established between the
Father above and the child below.
And who will measure the consola-
tions of the hour of prayer?

And immortality! Who will esti-
mate the peace which a belief in a future life has brought to the sorrowing
hearts of the sons of men? You may
talk to the young about death ending
all, for life is full and hope is strong,
but preach not this doctrine to the
mother who stands by the death-bed
of her babe or to one who is within
the shadow of a great affliction.
When I was a young man I wrote to

[46]

Colonel Ingersoll and asked him for his views on God and immortality. His secretary answered that the great infidel was not at home, but enclosed a copy of a speech of Colonel Ingersoll's which covered my question. I scanned it with eagerness and found that he had exprest himself about as follows: "I do not say that there is no God, I simply say I do not know. I do not say that there is no life beyond the grave, I simply say I do not know." And from that day to this I have asked myself the question and have been unable to answer it to my satisfaction, how could anyone find pleasure in taking from a human heart a living faith and substituting therefor the cold and cheerless doctrine, "I do not know."

Christ gave us proof of immortality and it was a welcome assurance,

[47]

altho it would hardly seem necessary
that one should rise from the dead to
convince us that the grave is not the
end. To every created thing God has
given a tongue that proclaims a future life.

If the Father deigns to touch with
divine power the cold and pulseless
heart of the buried acorn and to make
it burst forth from its prison walls,
will he leave neglected in the earth
the soul of man, made in the image
of his Creator? If he stoops to give
to the rose bush, whose withered
blossoms float upon the autumn
breeze, the sweet assurance of another springtime, will He refuse the
words of hope to the sons of men
when the frosts of winter come? If
matter, mute and inanimate, tho
changed by the forces of nature into
a multitude of forms, can never die,

will the imperial spirit of man suffer annihilation when it has paid a brief visit like a royal guest to this tenement of clay? No, I am sure that He who, notwithstanding his apparent prodigality, created nothing without a purpose, and wasted not a single atom in all his creation, has made provision for a future life in which man's universal longing for immortality will find its realization.

In Cairo I secured a few grains of wheat that had slumbered for more than thirty centuries in an Egyptian tomb. As I looked at them this thought came into my mind: If one of those grains had been planted on the banks of the Nile the year after it grew, and all its lineal descendants had been planted and replanted from that time until now, its progeny would to-day be sufficiently numerous to feed the teeming millions of the world. An unbroken chain of life connects the earliest grains of wheat with the grains that we sow and reap. There is in the grain of wheat an invisible something which has power to discard the body that we see, and from earth and air fashion a new body so much like the old one that we can not tell the one from the other. If this invisible germ of life in the grain of wheat can thus pass unimpaired through three thousand resurrections, I shall not doubt that my soul has power to clothe itself with a body suited to its new existence when this earthly frame has crumbled into dust. I am as sure that we live again as I am sure that we live to-day.

A belief in immortality not only consoles the individual, but it exerts a powerful influence in bringing peace between individuals. If one actually thinks that man dies as the brute dies, he will yield more easily to the temptation to do injustice to his neighbor when the circumstances are such as to promise security from detection. But if one really expects to meet again, and live eternally with, those whom he knows to-day, he is re-strained from evil deeds by the fear of endless remorse. We do not know what rewards are in store for us or what punishments may be reserved, but if there were no other it would be some punishment for one who deliberately and consciously wrongs another to have to live forever in the company of the person wronged and to have his littleness and selfishness laid bare. I repeat, a belief in immortality must exert a powerful influence in establishing justice between men and thus laying the foundation for peace.

Again, Christ deserves to be called the Prince of Peace because He has given us a measure of greatness which promotes peace. When His disciples quarreled among themselves as to which should be greatest in the Kingdom of Heaven, He rebuked them and said: "Let him who would be chiefest among you be the servant of all." Service is the measure of greatness; it always has been true; it is true to-day, and it always will be true, that he is greatest who does the most of good. And how this old world will be transformed when this standard of greatness becomes the standard of every life! Nearly all of our controversies and combats grow out of the fact that we are trying to get something from each other

—there will be peace when our aim is to do something for each other. Our enmities and animosities arise largely from our efforts to get as much as possible out of the world—there will be peace when our endeavor is to put as much as possible into the world. The human measure of a human life is its income; the divine measure of a life is its outgo, its overflow—its contribution to the welfare of all.

Christ also led the way to peace by giving us a formula for the propagation of truth. Not all of those who have really desired to do good have employed the Christian method—not all Christians even. In the history of the human race but two methods have been used. The first is the forcible method, and it has been employed most frequently. A man has an idea which he thinks is good; he tells his neighbors about it and they do not like it. This makes him angry; he thinks it would be so much better for them if they would like it, and, seizing a club, he attempts to make them like it. But one trouble about this rule is that it works both ways; when a man starts out to compel his neighbors to think as he does, he generally finds them willing to accept the challenge and they spend so much time in trying to coerce each other that they have no time left to do each other good.

The other is the Bible plan—"Be not overcome of evil but overcome evil with good." And there is no other way of overcoming evil. I am not much of a farmer—I get more credit for my farming than I should, and my little farm receives more advertising than it deserves. But I am farmer enough to know that if I cut down weeds they will spring up again; and farmer enough to know that if I plant something there which has more vitality than the weeds I shall not only get rid of the constant cutting, but have the benefit of the crop besides.

In order that there might be no mistake in His plan of propagating the truth, Christ went into detail and laid emphasis upon the value of example—"So live that others seeing your good works may be constrained to glorify your Father which is in Heaven." There is no human influence so potent for good as that which goes out from an upright life. A sermon may be answered; the arguments presented in a speech may be disputed, but no one can answer a

Christian life—it is the unanswerable
argument in favor of our religion.

It may be a slow process—this con-
version of the world by the silent influence of a noble example but it is
the only sure one, and the doctrine
applies to nations as well as to individuals. The Gospel of the Prince of
Peace gives us the only hope that the
world has—and it is an increasing
hope—of the substitution of reason
for the arbitrament of force in the
settlement of international disputes.
And our nation ought not to wait for
other nations—it ought to take the
lead and prove its faith in the omnip-
otence of truth.

But Christ has given us a platform so fundamental that it can be
applied successfully to all controversies. We are interested in platforms;
we attend conventions, sometimes

traveling long distances; we have wordy wars over the phraseology of various planks, and then we wage earnest campaigns to secure the endorsement of these platforms at the polls. The platform given to the world by the Prince of Peace is more far-reaching and more comprehensive than any platform ever written by the convention of any party in any country. When He condensed into one commandment those of the ten which relate to man's duty toward his fellows and enjoined upon us the rule, "Thou shalt love thy neighbor as thyself," He presented a plan for the solution of all the problems that now vex society or may hereafter arise. Other remedies may palliate or postpone the day of settlement, but this is all-sufficient and the reconciliation which it effects is a permanent one.

THE PRINCE OF PEACE

My faith in the future—and I have
faith—and my optimism—for I am
an optimist—my faith and my optimism rest upon the belief that
Christ's teachings are being more
studied to-day than ever before, and
that with this larger study will come a
larger application of those teachings
to the every-day life of the world, and
to the questions with which we deal.
In former times when men read that
Christ came "to bring life and immortality to light," they placed the
emphasis upon immortality; now they
are studying Christ's relation to human life. People used to read the
Bible to find out what it said of
Heaven; now they read it more to
find what light it throws upon the
pathway of to-day. In former years
many thought to prepare themselves
for future bliss by a life of seclusion

[58]

here; we are learning that to follow
in the footsteps of the Master we
must go about doing good. Christ
declared that He came that we might
have life and have it more abun-
dantly. The world is learning that
Christ came not to narrow life, but to
enlarge it—not to rob it of its joy, but
to fill it to overflowing with purpose,
earnestness and happiness.

But this Prince of Peace promises
not only peace but strength. Some
have thought His teachings fit only
for the weak and the timid and un-
suited to men of vigor, energy and
ambition. Nothing could be farther
from the truth. Only the man of
faith can be courageous. Confident
that he fights on the side of Jehovah,
he doubts not the success of his cause.
What matters it whether he shares
in the shouts of triumph? If every

word spoken in behalf of truth has its
influence and every deed done for
the right weighs in the final account,
it is immaterial to the Christian
whether his eyes behold victory or
whether he dies in the midst of the
conflict.

"Yea, tho thou lie upon the dust,
    When they who helped thee flee in fear,
Die full of hope and manly trust,
    Like those who fell in battle here.

Another hand thy sword shall wield,
    Another hand the standard wave,
Till from the trumpet's mouth is pealed,
    The blast of triumph o'er thy grave."

Only those who *believe* attempt the
seemingly impossible, and, by at-
tempting, prove that one, with God,
can chase a thousand and that two
can put ten thousand to flight. I can
imagine that the early Christians who

were carried into the coliseum to
make a spectacle for those more sav-
age than the beasts, were entreated
by their doubting companions not to
endanger their lives. But, kneeling
in the center of the arena, they prayed
and sang until they were devoured.
How helpless they seemed, and, meas-
ured by every human rule, how hopeless was their cause! And yet within
a few decades the power which they
invoked proved mightier than the
legions of the emperor and the faith
in which they died was triumphant
o'er all the land. It is said that those
who went to mock at their sufferings
returned asking themselves, "What is
it that can enter into the heart of man
and make him die as these die?"
They were greater conquerors in
their death than they could have been

had they purchased 'life by a surrender of their faith.

What would have been the fate of the church if the early Christians had had as little faith as many of our Christians have to-day? And if the Christians of to-day had the faith of the martyrs, how long would it be before the fulfilment of the prophecy that "every knee shall bow and every tongue confess"?

I am glad that He, who is called the Prince of Peace—who can bring peace to every troubled heart and whose teachings, exemplified in life, will bring peace between man and man, between community and community, between State and State, between nation and nation throughout the world—I am glad that He brings courage as well as peace so that those who follow Him may take up and

[62]

each day bravely do the duties that to that day fall.

As the Christian grows older he appreciates more and more the completeness with which Christ satisfies the longings of the heart, and, grateful for the peace which he enjoys and for the strength which he has received, he repeats the words of the great scholar, Sir William Jones:

"Before thy mystic altar, heavenly truth,
    I kneel in manhood, as I knelt in youth,
Thus let me kneel, till this dull form decay,
    And life's last shade be brightened by thy ray."

Printed in the USA
CPSIA information can be obtained
at www.ICGtesting.com
LVHW011137260524
781410LV00002B/597